The Rich Man and Lazarus

Literal History or Parable?

**An Advanced Study in Biblical psychology
carefully and lucidly expounded**

by

William Campbell

ISBN: 978-1-78364-280-9

**The Open Bible Trust
Fordland Mount, Upper Basildon,
Reading, RG8 8LU, GB.**

www.obt.org.uk

The Rich Man and Lazarus

Contents

1.
The Passage

The Passage

Luke 16:19-31

There was a certain rich man, which was clothed in purple and fine linen, and fared sumptuously every day: and there was a certain beggar named Lazarus, which was laid at his gate, full of sores, and desiring to be fed with the crumbs which fell from the rich man's table: moreover the dogs came and licked his sores.

And it came to pass, that the beggar died, and was carried by the angels into Abraham's bosom: the rich man also died, and was buried; and in hell he lift up his eyes, being in torments, and seeth Abraham afar off, and Lazarus in his bosom. And he cried and said,

> "Father Abraham, have mercy on me, and send Lazarus, that he may dip the tip of his finger in water, and cool my tongue; for I am tormented in this flame."

But Abraham said,

> "Son, remember that thou in thy lifetime receivedst thy good things, and likewise Lazarus evil things: but now he is comforted, and thou art tormented. And beside all this, between us and you there is a great gulf fixed: so that they which would pass from hence to you cannot; neither can they pass to us, that *would come* from thence."

Then he said,

"I pray thee therefore, father, that thou wouldest send him to my father's house: for I have five brethren; that he may testify unto them, lest they also come into this place of torment."

Abraham saith unto him,

"They have Moses and the prophets; let them hear them."

And he said,

"Nay, father Abraham: but if one went unto them from the dead, they will repent."

And he said unto him,

"If they hear not Moses and the prophets, neither will they be persuaded, though one rose from the dead."

2.
Introduction

Introduction

It is marvelous how the wisdom of God has wrought such problems into His Word, perplexing the mind, but gripping and holding the attention of each thoughtful reader; and in every successive generation providing inexhaustible sources of perennial interest. Our Lord spoke many simple sentences of heavenly wisdom, truth and grace; but sometimes He gave forth utterances hard to be understood; and this is one of the hardest. The question is, does this passage teach literal truth concerning man in death, or is it to be understood as a parable? In the minds of many who have sought to expound these verses, the unscriptural doctrine of the immortality of the human soul, and its ability to survive death as a separate conscious entity, widespread as it was, necessitated an understanding of the destiny of the righteous and the wicked. That the allegedly indestructible souls of the righteous should be taken to a place of bliss was an easy conception; but the necessity to understand some supposedly suitable fate for the souls of the unrighteous, misled expositors to fasten upon this and a few other passages of Scripture, and to make them indicate an eternity of conscious fiery torments of the unsaved.

In order to arrive at that conclusion it is necessary to understand this passage as a statement of literal truth, lifting the veil from the unseen, and depicting the state of the blessed dead and the torments of the cursed. But since the whole idea of the soul's natural immortality and consciousness in the death state, and of the eternal torments of the wicked is entirely contrary to the truth of God's Word, it is desirable that the fallacy of that interpretation of this passage should be eliminated from the minds of all who are or may become interested in these Divine themes; and that in place thereof a more Scriptural elucidation should be presented.

This work has been undertaken by numerous others; but the fathomless nature of the truth and riches of in one line of interpretation leave plenty of room for further endeavours.

3.
Cannot be Literal

Cannot be Literal

The obvious impossibility of taking this passage as literal truth becomes clear when tested. The Lord said that there was a certain rich man and there was a beggar. The beggar died, but nothing is said of his burial. He was carried by angels and placed in Abraham's bosom. Abraham, it will be remembered had died and had been buried in the cave of Machpelah (Gen. 25:8-10.) But Sarah also was buried there, and if anyone should be in Abraham's bosom, surely it would be Sarah his wife. It is impossible to avoid thinking how extraordinary it was that angels should take up the putrefying corpse of a beggar, covered with sores and doubtless clad in rags, and carry it some distance and place it beside the early patriarch. Also, it must have been an extremely unpleasant experience for Abraham, since, according to the passage, he was conscious of it.

The rich man also died, but he was buried; then, awaking as from a dream, he finds himself burning in a flame, although there is nothing else said about a fire in his sepulcher.

Against this perfectly reasonable rendering of the passage on the basis of a literal interpretation, it is argued, with the doctrine of the immortality of the soul in view, that it is to be understood that not the bodies of the parties concerned, but the souls, are meant, in the scene depicted in this passage. "Then it should read: And it came to pass that the beggar's body died and his soul was carried by the angels to the bosom of Abraham's soul; the rich man's body also died, and in hell he lifted up the eyes of his soul, being in torments, and seeth Abraham's soul afar off, and he cried and said, 'Father Abraham, have mercy on me, and send Lazarus' soul, that he may dip the tip of the finger of his soul in water and cool the tongue of my soul; for my soul is tormented in this flame'" ("Positive Theology." p. 160.)

This is a fair paraphrase of the passage, according to the interpretation of those who believe in the immortality of the soul and the eternal conscious torment of the souls of the unsaved dead; but it is a rendering which will not bear examination of the light of Holy Writ.

In the first place, the word "soul" does not once occur in the whole 13 verses of the passage; nor does the word "spirit," which is so often erroneously reckoned as synonymous with "soul."

In this second place, the written inspired Word of God in the days when the Lord gave forth this utterance, comprised the Old Testament Scriptures; and in all the 754 occurrences of the Hebrew word for soul ("nephesh"), the overwhelming testimony is against any possibility whatever of the soul surviving, in any form of conscious life, the death of the body.

In the third place, the abundant witness of the same Scriptures to the circumstances of the dead of mankind proves that they, being utterly helpless in the dreamless sleep of death, cannot possibly see, hear, feel, suffer, or speak to or communicate with each other, or with the living.

In the fourth place, while judgment to come beyond the conclusion of each individual's life on earth is taught in a few passages there is no indication that it will take place immediately after death; but rather that it will not be until resurrection, and in a far distant epoch of time.

And finally, the exit from death is resurrection; not survival by man's inherent ability in any form, but the exertion of the power of God to recall from the death state at His chosen time.[1]

---

[1] See book by the same author, "God's Gift of Everlasting Life" published by The Open Bible Trust.

4.
A Problem of Eschatology

A Problem of Eschatology

In coming to grips with this passage in Luke, it should be realised that while each single word of the passage is simple enough, the whole collection of its words constitutes what is probably the most complex problem in eschatology which the Bible contains. A thorough knowledge of its primary factors, and of others which impinge upon it, is essential.

Although there is no reference to the soul in the passage, a proper understanding of that term helps immensely in preserving a true focus of Scriptural light upon the subject. The Bible never designates the soul "immortal," or by any equivalent term; and its clear statements to the contrary preclude any possible inference to that effect. The clearest and shortest road to conviction of this truth is to study the 860 occurrences in a Hebrew-English Concordance of the word "nephesh" (soul) and in a Greek-English Concordance of the word "psuche" (soul). It is surprising, perhaps humiliating, to find that the lower creations were designated "souls" before man was created. This fact, and indeed the whole subject, is obscured by our English Bibles translating these Hebrew and Greek words by many other English words than "soul." The position is made clear in the following quotations: "God created great whales, and every living soul that moveth, which the waters brought forth" (Gen. 1:21); fishes are therefore "souls." Similarly, "A righteous man regardeth the soul of his beast" (Prov. 12:10).

When God breathed into man's nostrils the breath of life (Gen. 2:7), man, like the animals which had preceded him, became "a living soul" – not an immortal one. Breathing, animal life is the primary meaning of the word "soul"; and that life, or soul, reposes in the blood. "The soul of all flesh is the blood thereof" (Lev. 17:14). "And surely your blood of your souls will I require" (Gen. 9:5). In the development of human language the term "soul" became subject to some slight variation of usage: but in the Word of God the quality of immortality is never once attached to it. On the contrary, "The soul that sinneth, it shall die" (Ezek. 18:4); and, "He spared not their soul from death" (Psalm 78:50); and "The slayer that killeth any soul unawares" (Josh 20:3) – these and other passages definitely predicate the death of the soul.

And the death referred to is not "spiritual death"; it is a fundamental error to import, as some do, the advanced, figurative and evangelical language of Eph. 2:1 back into the Old Testament Scriptures. What death is could not be more plainly stated than in the language of God Himself in Gen. 3:19, "In the sweat of thy face shalt thou eat bread, till thou return unto the ground; for out of it wast thou taken; for dust thou art, and unto dust shalt thou return." "Thou" represents that which carries the personal identity; it came from dust at creation, and returns to dust when the breathing animal life expires, at death.

The soul reposes in the blood and is sustained by food; ". . . that which every soul must eat" (Ex. 12:16). It dies with the body and goes to the grave. Now, that the body goes to the grave needs no proof. "Ye shall bring down my grey hairs with sorrow to the grave," said Jacob (Gen. 44:29). The Hebrew word used here for "grave" is "Sheol," which occurs 65 times in the Old Testament; and the Greek word used to translate it into the Greek version of the Old Testament (the "Septuagint"), which was in common use when our Lord was on earth, is "Hades" – the very word used by the Lord of the place where the rich man found himself after death and burial. It does not signify any one particular tomb or sepulcher; but, in general, "gravedom," the place or state of the dead.

5.
Where the Soul Goes at Death

Where the Soul Goes at Death

But the Scriptures also clearly speak of the soul going there at death. "What man is he that liveth and shall not see death? Shall he deliver his soul from the hand of Sheol?" (Psalm 89:48). "His soul draweth near unto the grave" ("shakath," the pit of corruption). (Job 33:22.)

Now Sheol (Hades) is no place of bliss for the departed saint. "Great is Thy mercy toward me, and Thou hast delivered my soul from Sheol (Hades) beneath" (Psalm 86:13); that means that the Psalmist was preserved alive through some dangerous disease or risk of death.

Moreover, the death state is likened to a "sleep"; totally unconscious, inactive silent, helpless; this applies to saints and sinners alike. "Lighten mine eyes, lest I sleep the sleep of death" (Psalm 13:3). "Return, O Lord, deliver my soul; for in death there is no remembrance of Thee; in Sheol (Hades) who shall give Thee thanks?" (Psalm 6:4, 5). "Unless the Lord had been my help, my soul had quickly dwelt in silence" (Psalm 94:17). "Whatsoever thy hand findeth to do, do it with thy might; for there is no work, nor device, nor knowledge, nor wisdom in Sheol (Hades) whither thou goest" (Eccles. 9:10). "The living know that they shall die, but the dead know not anything" (Eccles 9:5). Nothing could be clearer than that the idea of the soul having existence independently of the body is distinctly repugnant to the use of the word in the inspired Scriptures.

But the Old Testament also teaches that the dead shall emerge from Sheol, the death state; not by inherent ability to survive death, but only by the exertion of God's almighty power to restore the dead to life. "Thou wilt not leave my soul in Sheol (Hades)" (Psalm 16:10); this is quoted by Peter on the Day of Pentecost (Acts 2:27) concerning the Lord Jesus Christ, not in support of His soul's survival, but in reference to His bodily resurrection. "Many of them that sleep in the dust of the earth shall awake, some to everlasting life, and some to shame and everlasting contempt" (Daniel 12:2); "Thou, which hast showed me great and sore troubles, shalt quicken me again and shalt bring me up again from the depths of the earth" (Psalm 71:20). Other passages of like import are found in Job 14:12; 19:25-27; Isaiah 26:19.

The Old Testament Scriptures have remarkably little to say regarding judgment after death. Daniel 12:2 already quoted refers to it, and Eccles. 12:14 indicates it.

The human spirit is primarily the breath. It is the very word used for "wind" (Hebrew "ruach"), and is the wind located in the nostrils and lungs. Secondarily, it is the fervour or other quality of the individual manner of life. The body, plus the spirit, becomes the "living soul." "Thou takest away their spirit (or breath), they die, and return to their dust" (Psalm 104:29). The spirit is never said to go to the grave (Sheol, Hades); but when the spirit expires, that which carries the individual identity (body, soul), goes there.

The New Testament does not contradict these fundamental truths taught in the Old Testament; it bears them out and amplifies them. But since the Old Testament alone existed when our Lord spoke the words of the passage before us, the evidence adduced above has been mostly limited to that portion of the Bible in order to demonstrate that the Lord Jesus – who would not for a moment contradict the inspired Word – could not possibly have intended that His words should be understood as teaching literal truth concerning the death state, when He spoke of the dead as being alive.

6.
It Must be
A Parable

It Must be a Parable

There is no alternative, therefore, but to consider Luke 16:19-31 as a parable[2]; and this it undoubtedly is. It is the last of a series of five parables, commencing with Luke 15:3, "And He spake this parable unto them, saying . . ." Then follows: The Parable of the Lost Sheep; and (v. 8), "Either what woman having ten pieces of silver . . ."' this is not termed a parable, but it is beyond doubt the Parable of the Lost Piece of Silver. Verse 11, and He said, "A certain man had two sons . . .": this reads like a statement of literal truth, but it is beyond controversy, the Parable of the Lost Son. 16:1. "And He said also unto His disciples, **There was a certain rich man . . .**"; here are the very same words which introduce to us "The Rich Man and Lazarus"; but it is the Parable of the Unjust Steward or the Parable of the Lost Employment. And finally, v. 19, "There was a certain rich man . . ."; the parable of the Lost Favour of God.

But the drapery of the parable is not that of the Old Testament Scriptures. It is not even based on what could actually occur, as the previous four parables are based. Did not then the Lord seriously risk being misunderstood? In the very first parable in the Bible (Judges 9:7-15), Jotham speaks without explanation or apology of trees talking to one another. Would not his hearers be misled into thinking he meant that trees could speak? No, of course not. Common sense and experience would give them to understand without the slightest difficulty that he was speaking in a parable, and not meaning that trees could actually speak. So also here; when the Lord spoke of the dead talking to one another, and a flame of suffering in the death state, **Scripture** sense would

---

[2] For more on parables see "The Purpose of Parables" by Michael Penny, published by The Open Bible Trust.

give those who knew the Word of God (and all His hearers ought to have known it), to understand without the slightest difficulty that He was speaking in a parable, and not meaning that the dead could actually speak; for the only Scripture then extant (the Old Testament), abundantly showed this to be impossible. And it is only those who take the place of the Pharisees and ignore and disbelieve the Old Testament testimony on the state of the dead who are in any way misled.

The clothing of the parable is found in the traditions of the scribes and Pharisees, already existing abundantly in our Lord's day. "Full well ye reject the commandment of God, that ye may keep your tradition" (Mark 7:9). In this parable the Lord, without saying so, was taking one of their traditions, in which they had rejected the revelation of the inspired Scriptures, and He was turning it against themselves. If it be said that this would result in mystification both to them and to us, then there is perceived here another deep principle of our Lord's words. His deeper teachings presuppose a careful knowledge of the written Word of God; He never excuses ignorance on the part of those who ought to know. Remember how He mystified Nicodemus (John 3:1-12) and chided him for not perceiving the bearing of the Old Testament Scriptures upon His words, although He did not quote the Scriptures in explanation. Nor did He stop to make His meaning clear to those who bitterly opposed him; on the contrary, He deliberately entangled them further, with more difficult sayings still. In John 6, the Jews "murmured at Him" (v. 41), and "strove among themselves" v. 52) over His words. But the Lord did not mollify them with explanations; instead, He spoke more difficult words still, so that "from that time many of His disciples went back, and walked no more with Him" (v. 66).

7.
The Series of Five Parables

The Series of Five Parables

The first three parables of this series of five were called forth from the Lord in His compassion towards publicans and sinners (15:1), and to draw them nearer to Him who came to seek and to save that which was lost. The reason for the last two arose from the presence of the Pharisees and scribes (15:2), who murmured at the beginning of the series and derided ("turned up their noses") towards the end. The Parable of the Unfaithful Steward was spoken against the scribes and Pharisees. "who devour widows' houses, and for a pretense make long prayers; therefore ye shall receive the greater condemnation" (Mark 12:40). Their unfaithfulness in money matters was shown in the parable as in a mirror, but they mocked Him. It was this obdurate, incorrigible impenitence which called forth this very strong statement from the lips of the Lord, embodied in the Parable of the Rich Man and Lazarus. The clue to the inner meaning of the whole passage lies in the words: "Ye are they which justify yourselves before men, but God knoweth your hearts."

It is no surprise that these Pharisees should not have been cautioned against any misunderstanding. The Lord Himself gives a reason why they were addressed in parables, even "because they, seeing, see not and hearing hear not, neither do they understand . . . for this people's heart is waxed gross and their ears are dull of hearing, and their eyes have closed; lest at any time they should see with their eyes, and hear with their ears, and understand with their heart, and should be converted and I should heal them"; "THEREFORE SPEAK I TO THEM IN

PARABLES" (Matt. 13:13-15). In this parable therefore, we have this principle in operation to its fullest extent.

8.

Jewish Erroneous Traditions

Jewish Erroneous Traditions

From all this it seems perfectly clear that the Lord was not setting forth these things concerning the Rich Man in Hades and torment, and the Beggar in Abraham's Bosom, as a parable of His own invention, or as His own direct teaching; but that He was taking the current traditional teachings of the Pharisees, which He was condemning and using them against themselves, thus convicting them out of their own mouths.

In the Jewish Commentaries on the Old Testament Scriptures, such traditions abounded. Here is one of them from a commentary on Exodus:

> "There was a good man and a wicked man that died; as for the good man, he had no funeral rites solemnized, but the wicked man had. Afterward, there was one who saw in his dream, the good man walking in the gardens and hard by pleasant springs; but the wicked man, with his tongue trickling drop by drop, at the bank of a river, endeavouring to touch the water but he could not."

In a commentary on Ecclesiastes we are told that (as to the "great gulf"),

> "God hath set the one against the other; that is, Gehenna and Paradise. How far are they distant? A hand-breadth, Jochanan saith, A wall is between. But the Rabbis say, They are so even with one another that they may see out

of one into the other." (From "The Rich Man and Lazarus," by Dr. Bullinger.)

Similar traditions are common to heathen nations, but foreign to the truth of the Bible. It would be impossible for us to suppose for a moment that Christ could be teaching here that which is the very opposite to the whole Word of God.

And what insuperable difficulty can there be in the way of supposing that our Lord chose to embody the lessons He would teach in a story framed out of such well-known ideas as those held by the Pharisees? In the parable of the servants (Luke 19:11-27) we have another example of the Lord using the thoughts of others, without endorsing them, but to the condemnation of those who held them. "Out of thine own mouth will I judge thee, thou wicked servant. Thou knewest that I was an austere man …" The Lord does not consent to the accusation of being a hard man, but He so employs the man's own idea and weaves his words to his condemnation. In Matt. 12:27 the Lord answered the Pharisees who accused Him of casting out demons by Beelzebub. "If I by Beelzebub cast out devils, by whom do your children cast them out? therefore they shall be your judges." He did not stop to refute their false notion, but turned it against them. In Matt. 9:10-13 the Pharisees found fault with the Lord for "eating with publicans and sinners." "But when Jesus heard that, He said unto them, 'They that be whole need not a physician, but they that be sick . . . For I am not come to call the righteous, but sinners to repentance.'" The Pharisees thought they were righteous and the Lord appeared to take them at their own valuation, but showed them that they thereby excluded themselves from the blessings He came to bestow.

9.
What Does
This Parable Mean?

What Does This Parable Mean?

The Parable of the Rich Man and Lazarus, therefore, is only one of quite a number of occasions when the Lord took the erroneous ideas of the Pharisees apparently at their face value, but left His hearers with considerations of the most serious import to ponder.

Now, since it has not seemed good to the Holy Spirit to leave on record for our enlightenment any written explanation of this parable, and we do not even know that any oral explanation was given to the disciples, such as our Lord gave to the apostles concerning the Parables of the Sower and the Tares (Matt. 13:10-23; 36-43), and yet the parable itself is written down for our learning, we are left to exercise our spiritual understanding to grasp the mind of the Lord in the words which He spoke. This, therefore, is now humbly attempted.

It would appear, first of all, that there is an intensive significance, intended to impress the Pharisees at that time. The parable is essentially Jewish; it was spoken to and directed specifically towards the Pharisees (v. 14, 15). It was before the great transaction of the Cross; and is to be understood, not in the light of the great Gospel unfoldings given years later in Romans and Hebrews, but in the atmosphere of "Moses and the prophets" already in the possession of the hearers.

> **There was a certain rich man, which was clothed in purple and fine linen, and fared sumptuously every day."**

From the fate of the rich man in the parable we infer that he had lived without the favour of God, but it is remarkable that the Lord says nothing at all about his moral or spiritual state. Riches, fine linen and sumptuous fare do not of themselves constitute a man a "hell-deserving sinner." Abraham himself was rich, so was Joseph, and Moses in Egypt, and David and Solomon. So also in the New Testament were Joseph of Arimathea, and Nicodemus, and Philemon. It is not even said that this rich man was remiss in his duty to his poor brother Lazarus (according to Deut. 15:7), who desired to be fed from the rich man's crumbs – we are not told whether he was so fed or not.

Now many of the Pharisees were covetous (v. 14), and they reckoned riches to be God's hallmark upon their righteousness, in accordance with Deut. 28:1-8. They evidently reckoned these promised blessings to be individual (despite the state of Israel at large), rather than national, and dependent upon the majority of the nation observing the conditions. They were blind to the fact that the nation's wickedness had "turned things upside down" (Isaiah 29:13-16), and that Psalm 73:12 was more like a true reflection of the spiritual state of the nation: "Behold, these are the ungodly, who prosper in the world; they increase in riches." (See also Luke 6:24). That this hallucination persisted in the minds of the common people also is the explanation of the disciples' amazement in Matt. 19:25, "Who then can be saved?"

10.
The Significance
of a
Name

The Significance of a Name

"And there was a certain beggar name Lazarus."

The rich man was not given a name, but the beggar receives one. It has been argued that this must be narrative because the beggar has been given a name, making the statement one of actual circumstance. But why should not a parabolic character be given a name if it serves the speaker's purpose? If the prodigal son had been named Benjamin, would that necessarily have transformed the parable into historic narrative? Surely not. And it did serve the Lord's purpose remarkably well, for He would know what was coming to pass in the death and resurrection of Lazarus; the brother of Martha and Mary; and the force of the name in the parable is perceived when we connect the concluding words, Neither will they be persuaded though one rose from the dead," with the fact that this saying, and the actual raising of Lazarus from the dead, could not have been far removed from one another in point of time. 'Neither will they be persuaded . . ." and later we read **"but the chief priests consulted that they might put Lazarus also to death."** (John 12:10.)

It is not necessarily to be assumed that the beggar was a pious man, though his destiny indicates that he did come into God's favour; but the description of his condition before death has no savour of a Godly life, but rather the opposite.

Both men died, and each is thereupon represented as finding himself alive; one in woe in torturing flame, the other in comfort.

But that is contrary to Eccles. 3:19-20, which states the very humbling truth that the lower creation and man in death "all go unto one place; all are of the dust, and all turn to dust again"; but it is agreeable to the traditions of the Pharisees, as reflected in Josephus' "Discourse on Hades,"[3] where we read that "Hades, wherein the souls of the righteous and unrighteous are detained . . . is a place in the world not regularly finished; a subterraneous region." There is a descent to this region, with a gate, at which stands an archangel, and a host of angels, who guide the souls of the just to the right hand, where they enjoy the prospect of the good things they see, and the smiles of the fathers and of the just, while they await their eternal abode in heaven. "This place we call **The Bosom of Abraham**."

"But as to the unjust, they are dragged by force to the left hand by angels allotted for punishment . . . into the neighbourhood of hell itself . . . a terrible and exceeding great prospect of fire . . . where they see the place of the fathers and of the just, even hereby are they punished; for a chaos deep and large is fixed between them; insomuch that a just man that hath compassion upon them cannot . . . pass over it." Here is the imagery of the Lord's parable.

The beggar is not said to have been buried, or to have gone to Hades at all, but was carried by the angels to Abraham's Bosom, where he was within sight and hearing of Hades, where the rich man found himself in torment. In all the Old Testament teaching concerning Sheol there is no such teaching as "two compartments" there; one for the good and the other for the evil. Such an expression as "the lowest hell" (Psalm 86:13) simply means "Sheol beneath." Out of the 65 occurrences of Sheol only once is fire connected therewith; and even then not as to the

---

[3] See the Appendix where this is reproduced in full.

punishment of the dead, but judgment on the living (Deut. 32:22). That passage will be considered later herein.

11.
Gehenna
is *Not* in View

Gehenna is *Not* in View

It may be remarked here that the teaching concerning "Gehenna" ("Hell-fire") in the New Testament is quite a different subject from that concerning Hades. Strange to say, the references to Gehenna are strictly limited to the nation of Israel. Paul, the Apostle to the Gentiles, could say, "I am pure from the blood of all men, for I have not shunned to declare unto you all the counsel of God" (Acts 20:26-27); yet in all his writings and reported speeches the word "Gehenna" does not once occur. It has nothing to do with the thought of the eternal torment of lost souls' it is for destruction, not for preservation.

If fire is once connected with Sheol, so also is water; for Jonah, in the stomach of the great fish, far down in ocean depths, said, "Out of the belly of Sheol cried I, and Thou heardest my voice. For Thou hadst cast me into the deep, in the midst of the seas" (Jonah 2:2, 3).

The rich man sees and recognises Abraham afar off, and Lazarus there also; he cries to Abraham. begging that Lazarus be sent with a drop of water on his fingertip to cool his tongue. Now it is true that in Isaiah 14:9-11, 15-17, and in Ezek. 32:21 the dead are represented as speaking to others who are joining them in the grave. This idea, being entirely contrary to the abundant teaching of the Old Testament on the state of the dead, must be figurative language; and these passages therefore provide some Scriptural basis for the imagery of the highly figurative language of this parable in Luke 16.

"Father Abraham, have mercy on me . . . for I am tormented in this flame," cries the rich man. (Here is the only instance in Scripture of a prayer address to a dead saint, and it utterly failed of any help. The Bible gives no justification for prayers to the dead; not even to the Virgin Mary!)

But Abraham said, "Son, remember that thou in thy lifetime receivedst thy good things and likewise Lazarus evil things; but now he is comforted and thou art tormented." There is not one word of accusation here as to sin. Abraham did not even say **"Therefore** thou are tormented." Taking it literally, it becomes a travesty of all reason to reckon that a person receiving good things in this life is to suffer fiery torments after death; and a person receiving evil things here and now is to be comforted after he dies. Abraham said, "Son, remember"; but the Scripture clearly shows this to be impossible. "in death there is no remembrance of Thee" (Psalm 6:5); and if there be no remembrance there of God, who or what else will be remembered? The truth is that "there is no knowledge in the grave" (Eccles. 9:10), and no remembrance; all is silent and still. It is "the land of forgetfulness" (Psalm 88:12).

"And beside all this, between us and you there is a great gulf fixed." Old Testament evidence knows nothing of it. For instance, Rehoboam, a wicked king, the son of Solomon and grandson of David, died, and "slept with his fathers" (2 Chron. 12:14-16). There could have been no "great gulf fixed" therefore between David and Solomon on the one hand and Rehoboam on the other. And like expressions are used of other kings of Israel and Judah, good and bad without discrimination. Even Abraham himself was "gathered to his people" (Gen. 25:8), and they were idolaters (Josh. 24:2).

12.
No Warnings of Future Torture

No Warnings of Future Torture

The subsequent dialogue between the rich man and Abraham raises considerations of the utmost importance in the interpretation of this passage. The rich man, finding himself in a place of fiery torment after death, desires that his five brethren should be warned in time against a like fate. The words put into Abraham's mouth clearly indicate that the writings of Moses and the prophets contained sufficient testimony and warning; but the remarkable thing is that in the whole of the Old Testament there is not one word to warn the living that after they die they will, if they have received good things in this life, find themselves alive in Sheol in fiery torment; nor is there one word to give warning that if they die away from the favour of God they will find themselves in such a case; nor even if they are the wickedest possible sinners at the moment they die, will they awake in Sheol in flame. Nothing is revealed in the Old Testament of body, soul or spirit suffering punishment in the death state.

If this passage in Luke is literal truth, therefore, the rich man would have a clear case against the justice of heaven. Throughout the Old Testament the legal position between God and man is substantially the same as said at the beginning to Adam in Gen. 2:17. "In the day that thou eatest thereof, thou shalt surely die": that is, the judgment upon sin is death, not fiery torment in a conscious death state. The infliction of death may be with more or less pain; but death, which is the result of the cessation of life, ends all suffering. The awful sinners of Sodom "suffered the vengeance of eternal fire" (Jude 7); they were burnt alive, but death completely ended their sufferings, and the fire itself has long ago gone out; indeed, the Dead Sea probably covers the spot today.

Even the more fearful sinners of a coming day (Rev. 14:9-11), who will worship the Beast and wear his mark, are warned already by the written Word, and will have the warning specially carried to them by angelic announcement, of judgment in fiery torment; yet they will be human beings in the flesh, whose torment must end at last in death. The torment of the locusts (Rev. 9:5-6), is made more fearful because the refuge of death is temporarily denied; yet a warning already stands written in the Bible against that day, and the duration of the infliction is limited to five months.

But where in "Moses and the Prophets" was this rich man warned of fiery flame and torment in the death state, to follow a certain course of life in the flesh? From Genesis to Malachi there is no such warning. It is impossible that this passage can be taken to teach any such doctrine as the torment of the dead in the death state, whether temporary or eternal. Otherwise the justice of God is at stake; and it is very wrong exegesis which founds, upon a difficult and unexplained parable, such a doctrine as would contradict the plain and abundant statements of Scripture on the subject.

13.
Death is a
Sleep

Death is a Sleep

And the New Testament Scriptures, given after this parable was spoken, and including the fullest revelation of the whole counsel of God given to mankind, agree with the Old Testament teaching on this weighty theme. The death state is a sleep[4]. "Our friend Lazarus sleepeth" (John 11:11); not that his body sleeps and his soul is conscious somewhere else; but the one indivisible man, Lazarus, sleeps in death; and the exit therefrom is not by survival of the soul (or spirit), but by the resurrection of the dead by the exertion of almighty power; and that not individual, but in groups; for example, we read in 1 Cor. 15:22-24, ". . . so in Christ shall all be made alive. But every man in his own order; Christ the first fruits; afterward they that are Christ's at His coming. Then cometh the end."

And after resurrection comes judgment – that is, for the unsaved. "And I saw a Great White Throne . . . and I saw the dead, small and great stand before God . . . and Death and Hades delivered up the dead which were in them; and they were judged every man according to his works." Sentence and punishment follow resurrection and judgment. No one is punished before he is judged; but there is no indication either of resurrection or trial or judgment in the case of this rich man.

And finally, the doctrine of the Old Testament and of the New is that the wages of sin is death; sinners have been suddenly cut off for their sins by the infliction of the first death; that is frequently found in the Old Testament, and is threatened in the New also; but the New Testament reveals the resurrection of the wicked

---

[4] For more on this see "Asleep in Christ" by Helaine Burch, published by The Open Bible Trust.

dead, and the judgment of the Great White Throne, and the infliction of the Second Death upon those whose names are not found in the Book of Life – but the infliction is **death** – not life in misery.

But the rich man in the parable desired some warning more striking than the written Word to be sent to his five brothers.

"If one went unto them from the dead, they will repent." But this also was denied by Abraham; and when the literal Lazarus went from the dead back among his fellows, and all the Jews far and near heard about him (John 12:10, 11), the chief priests, instead of believing on the Lord Jesus Christ by the testimony of "one from the dead," consulted how to quench his testimony.

And Abraham said unto him, "If they hear not Moses and the prophets, neither will they be persuaded, though one rose from the dead." The Lord Jesus rose from the dead; and while He did not appear to any but His friends, the powerful testimony of His resurrection was proclaimed by the Apostles with the power of the Holy Spirit, and many thousands believed; but the rulers of the Jews did their utmost to quench their testimony also; first of all by bribing the officers left to guard the tomb, to tell a lie (Matt. 28:11-15), and then by imprisonment, by stripes, by persecution and scattering, and by slaughter – especially under Saul the Pharisee, incited by his fellow Pharisees, some of whom may have heard this parable at the lips of our Lord.

14.

What Does this Parable Teach?

What Does the Parable Teach?

The elucidatory discussions of the parable making clear what it does **not** teach, prepare the way for an attempt to understand our Lord's intention. Certain powerful lessons would be driven home to the minds of the immediate listeners:

1) The covetous Pharisees to whom the Lord spoke this parable evidently considered themselves righteous men, and reckoned that their wealth constituted a manifest token of God's favour, and a pledge of felicity in the life to come. The Lord had publicly said at the beginning of His ministry, "That except your righteousness shall exceed the righteousness of the scribes and Pharisees, ye shall in no case enter into the kingdom of heaven" (Matt. 5:20); and again, "How hard is it for them that trust in riches to enter into the kingdom of God!" (Mark 10:24). This parable strongly emphasised these statements. The Lord thus reminded them that the superficial aspect of this present life does not necessarily indicate the reckoning of God, Who looks not upon the outward appearance but upon the heart.

2) The parable vividly indicated that the end of this present life closes all opportunity to change one's destiny; and therefore that true wisdom lies in tearing away all self-deception and making quite sure of an acceptable walk before God here and now; otherwise there lies before them "a certain fearful looking for of fiery indignation" (Heb. 10:27). This constituted another call to repentance.

3) The parable taught that the written Word of God is sufficient for all necessary guidance and prompting in the way of eternal blessedness.

4) It anticipated the state of hardened and persistent incredulity and enmity on the Pharisees' part towards the witness of the Apostles to the resurrection of the Lord Himself.

15.
Repentant Sinners versus Pharisees

Repentant Sinners versus Pharisees

These lessons had application to the Lord's immediate hearers; but it is probable that this profound utterance is intended to yield more extensive interpretations. At the beginning of the series of five parables (Luke 15:1, 2) we find mention of a class of Jews whom the Pharisees despised and whose spiritual condition answered exactly to the beggar's physical state. "full of sores." Isaiah described them (Isaiah 1:4-6), "Ah sinful nation, a people laden with iniquity," full of "wounds and bruises and putrefying sores."

Now the Israelites looked down upon the Gentiles as dogs. Even our Lord used this term of the Gentile woman (Matt. 15:26), though He tempered it by using the diminutive "puppy dogs," and used it for a very gracious purpose. And the dogs which licked the beggar's sores may represent the Romans who kept the Jewish sinners in order, and preserved some semblance of peace.

The rich man addresses Abraham as "Father"; this agrees with their proud claim in John 8:33, "We be Abraham's seed"; which claim John the Baptist anticipated and answered in Matt. 3:9, "And think not to say within yourselves, we have Abraham to our father, for I say unto you that God is able of these stones to raise up children unto Abraham." Thrice the rich man thus addresses Abraham; but only once, and that the first time, does Abraham acknowledge the relationship in the word "Son." In his other two replies this acknowledgment is omitted.

But these sinful Jews were hearkening to the gracious invitation to "Come now and let us reason together, saith the Lord; though your sins be as scarlet, they shall be as white as snow" (Isaiah 1:18). "Then drew near unto Him all the publicans and sinners for to hear Him" (Luke 15:1); evidently, like Zaccheus, with real spiritual hunger after a restoration to righteousness and the blessing of God. It was to them that the beautiful, tender and gracious parables of the Lost Sheep, the Lost Coin and the Lost Son were spoken, with the heart-touching visions of a seeking Shepherd and a tender-hearted and forgiving Father. Many such hearers had believed, and had secured from God by their faith in His Son the certainty of eternal life and blessedness in the coming Kingdom, for the Lord had said, "Verily I say unto you, that the publicans and the harlots go into the Kingdom of God before you. For John came unto you in the way of righteousness, and ye believed him not; but the publicans and the harlots believed him." (Matt. 21:31, 32).

Thus the beggar had attained to the true place of relationship to Abraham which the rich man had lost. And with regard to the beggar being "comforted," it is remarkable that when the Romans besieged and destroyed Jerusalem in A.D. 70 with great slaughter, and the scattering of its Jewish inhabitants who escaped the sword, all the Jewish Christians escaped from the city before its final capture, and saved their lives, because they believed the Lord's words in Luke 21:20-22, while the unbelieving Jews "fell by the edge of the sword or were led away captive into all nations" (v. 24) – into the flame of the torment.

Now the Kingdom of God is not some compartment in Hades, nor in the death state at all, nor is it the Church; it is the reign of Christ on earth in the Millennium, when the Lord Jesus returns to earth and sits upon "the Throne of the Lord" (1 Chron. 29:23) in Jerusalem, and rules over all the earth in righteousness and peace and blessing. The reference to the beggar being "carried by the angels into Abraham's bosom" strikingly recalls the Lord's words in Matt. 24:31, "And He shall send His angels with a great sound of a trumpet, and they shall gather together His elect from the four winds, from one end of heaven to the other." These will then be among those referred to in Matt. 8:11. "And I say unto you, that many shall come from the east and west, and shall sit down with Abraham and Isaac and Jacob, in the kingdom of heaven." But the proud unrepentant Pharisees would be among those referred to in v. 12, "But the children of the kingdom shall be cast out into outer darkness; there shall be weeping and gnashing of teeth."

By that time the "great gulf" between them will indeed be fixed, and the weeping and gnashing of teeth will be unrelieved by any "drop of water" from those who inherit the Kingdom; for that punishment is of God. If, however, those upon whom it is inflicted "lift up their eyes" as they are about to enter into Hades, and send forth one plea for personal relief, or at least for the deliverance of their friends, it can only be for one brief moment before their torment ends in the oblivion of death; for it will assuredly end there.

These five parables are compressed into a nutshell in Luke 18:9-14, in the parable of the self-righteous Pharisee in the Temple justifying himself before God, and the repentant publican who would not so much as lift his eyes up to heaven, but smote upon his breast and said, "God be merciful to me, a sinner."

16.
Israel
versus
The Gentiles

Israel versus The Gentiles

A great difficulty with this parable of the rich man and Lazarus, however, is the impossibility of finding any one interpretation into which all the details of the drapery of the parable will fit. In the last-mentioned exegesis, the difficulty is that those carried by the angels and those cast out are not the dead, but people living in flesh and blood when that time comes. Now we cannot think that the various details are brought into our Saviour's discourses idly, but must assuredly have some divine significance. There may, therefore, have been in the Lord's intention other lines of interpretation, equally applicable and each embodying some feature which other interpretations cannot incorporate.

In the rich man we may see an accurate representation of the nation of Israel as a whole; chosen of God, called to be His "peculiar treasure above all people . . . a kingdom of priests and an holy nation" (Exodus 19:5, 6). Their great spiritual privileges were later summed up by the Apostle Paul (Romans 9:4, 5) ". . . Who are Israelites; to whom pertaineth the adoption, and the glory, and the covenants . . . whose are the fathers, and of whom as concerning the flesh Christ" was to come. Their kings were clothed in purple and their priests in fine linen. Their material blessings, also, in the promises of God, were immense, providing all that heart could wish. "The Lord shall command the blessing upon thee in thy storehouses . . . and the Lord shall make thee plenteous in goods . . . the Lord shall open unto thee His good treasure . . . (Deut. 28:1-14).

But the rest of the world were well represented by the beggar Lazarus. Their fearful spiritual degradation is described in Romans 1:18-32. In the civilized but pagan nations in Asia Minor, Greece and Rome in our Lord's day, law, philosophy, art and military prowess flourished side by side with abominable profligacy; from which not a few of the nobler minded of the Gentiles turned with loathing, and sought in the religion of Israel to find something much more satisfying, by its doctrine of one omnipotent God (instead of the 30,000 gods of the Greeks) Who was holy, pure and good, whereas the gods of these nations were the very opposite. Such Gentiles were found in the Jewish synagogues by Paul in many cities; such Gentiles came to Christ Himself for "crumbs" of the good things He was then giving to Israel; the centurion (Matt. 8:5), the Canaanitish woman (Matt. 15:22), the Greeks (John 12:20), and others. The Gentiles might then be said to be alive, seeking crumbs of spiritual help, but when the full Gospel came, proclaiming redemption through the blood of Jesus Christ, the truth was then revealed that they were as good as dead; "If one died for all, then were all dead" (2 Cor. 5:14).

During the period of the Book of the Acts, therefore, we see the outlines of the fulfilment of the parable, in its reversal of the spiritual conditions of Israel and of the Gentiles. "Many of the Corinthians (Gentiles) hearing, believed, and were baptised" (Acts 18:8); many of whom were drunkards, thieves, idolaters, and covetous and immoral persons of the worst type (1 Cor. 6:9-11). They were dead in sins, but quickened by the Spirit, they were made alive in Christ spiritually; and dispensationally they were in "Abraham's Bosom." "If ye be Christ's, then are ye Abraham's seed, and heirs according to the promise" (Gal. 3:29). They awoke and found themselves "blessed with faithful Abraham" (Gal. 3:9). But they have not entered with Abraham upon the promised blessings yet; for Abraham, and all the patriarchs and heroes of Heb. 11 died without having "received the fulfilment of the promise." Abraham has not yet received the Land of Canaan promised to him; nor has he entered the New Jerusalem (Heb. 11:10, 16), revealed to him; for David was still in his grave ten days after our Lord's ascension (Acts 2:34), and not taken from Hades to heaven with the ascending Lord, as some aver concerning the Old Testament saints; but like all the Lord's people in every dispensation of the past and present, if they die, they await the resurrection of the dead, as indicated in general in the words, "they that are Christ's, at His Coming" (1 Cor. 15:23).

But the Israelites by birth – represented by the rich man – who believed not the Gospel, were heirs of impending wrath. "They please not God and are contrary to all men; forbidding us to speak to the Gentiles, that they might be saved, to fill up their sins alway; for the wrath is come upon them to the uttermost" (1 Thess. 2:15, 16).

17.
Israel
"Died and
was Buried"

Israel "Died and was Buried"

At the destruction of Jerusalem in A.D. 70 the nation of Israel may well be said to have "died." In fact, this very thought is borne out by the vision of the "dry bones" (Ezekiel 37). "These bones are the whole House of Israel . . . Thus saith the Lord, Behold, O my people, I will open your graves and cause you to come up out of your graves, and bring you into the land of Israel" (v. 12). They are buried among the nations of the world; yet very much alive, and in torment; and the flame of their torment is the fire kindled in God's anger, referred to in Deut. 32:22. In fact the words of the immediate context of that passage are quoted in Rom. 10:19 as explanatory of the dispensational state of Israel during the Book of Acts; and the "fire" was even then impending; "they shall be burnt with hunger, and devoured with burning heat, and with bitter destruction . . . the sword without, and terror within, shall destroy . . ." Their torment is fearfully enlarged upon in Deut. 28:15-68: diseases, oppressions, vexations, frustrations, pestilences; scattering, wandering, contempt, sorrow, sufferings, and death. During the long centuries since Jerusalem was destroyed these curses have in some measure been suffered by them; but their full measure will be endured during "The Day of the Lord"; that period of the Book of Revelation of Jesus Christ (which is the prophetic succession to the historical Book of the Acts), when the present parenthesis of the Church the Body of Christ is completed (during which the "great gulf" has been bridged by the Cross of Christ, so that there is recognised no distinction whatever between Jew and Gentile), and the Church is removed to the heavens and God takes up once more with His ancient people Israel, and with the nations as such, to lead earth's affairs swiftly onward to their crisis at Armageddon, and their consummation in the glorious millennial reign of Christ, when all the promises to Abraham will be fulfilled.

18.
Jews in Palestine versus Jews Outside

Jews in Palestine versus Jews Outside

But consideration of the details of the parable lead to another line of application. In the Roman campaign resulting in the destruction of Jerusalem, it was the Jews in Palestine who directly suffered. These may be viewed as represented by the rich man himself. But many more of the same nation were outside of that land, scattered in all the surrounding countries enumerated in Acts 2:5-11. These would be represented by the "five brethren." The rich man begs that Lazarus be sent to his five brethren, warning them of the peril into which he himself had fallen: but his request is denied, with the explanation that the Scriptures are sufficient for them, and that even such a sign as one risen from the dead would not of itself convince them of the error of their ways, to lead them into the paths of righteousness, and of felicity in the life to come.

The foresight of this answer is echoed in 1 Cor. 1:22, 23: "The Jews require a sign, and the Greeks seek after wisdom; but we preach Christ crucified unto the Jews a stumbling block, and unto the Greeks foolishness." The Apostle Paul had gone among them, in city after city, where "Moses . . . was read in the synagogues every sabbath day" (Acts 15:21) proclaiming One risen from the dead, upholding his proclamation by the manifestation of God's power, in signs, and wonders, and miracles; yet still he had to record that "The Jews require a sign"; their perversity demanding any sign but those divinely appointed. "Master, we would see a sign from Thee." had said scribes and Pharisees to the Lord (Matt. 12:38) after many signs had already been given which they would not believe. Their request was denied. "If He be the King of Israel, let Him now come down from the cross and we will believe Him," said our Lord's murders (Matt. 27:42); but this also was denied them. The "five brethren" – the Jews of the Dispersion – were of the same stubborn nature as the "rich man" himself – the Jews in the Land. So the answer in the parable was given. "Neither will they be persuaded, though one rose from the dead."

19.
The Love and
Justice
of God

The Love and Justice of God

In conclusion, the following points remain to be emphasised. The whole Scripture teaching concerning the soul is in line with the original explanation of man's creation; "The Lord God formed man of the dust of the ground, and breathed into his nostrils the breath of life; and man became a living soul" (Gen. 2:7). "The Old Testament throughout never departs from the opening statement, nor can it fairly be said that anywhere in its contents is there a text which declares that man is now the possessor of a "soul" or "spirit," which is the real man within the body, and able to live and carry consciousness when the body is dead. When the New Testament opens there is no statement to be met with which opposes this conclusion furnished for us by the elder Scriptures. Man is still viewed as a mortal, perishing creature, entirely dependent upon God for his life. The teaching brought by Jesus Christ tells of a "gift" which is designed to meet man's need at this point" (quoted from the late Pastor G. Aldridge).

The state of the dead, both good and bad, is properly described in both Old and New Testaments as a sleep; it is total unconsciousness. The rich man is not said to go into Gehenna ("hell fire"), but Hades ("the grave"); Lazarus is not permitted to go from the death state to the living with any message at all. Incidentally, the parable gives no justification whatever for the doctrines and practice of Spiritualism.

The Scripture doctrine of retribution demands judgment and sentence before execution; that is simple justice. The fate of the rich man in the parable cannot possible be a picture of the unsaved being cast, in any shape or form, into fiery torments at the moment of death. The Bible plainly declares that the unjust are reserved unto the Day of Judgment to be punished (2 Peter 2:9); and that day is after the Millennium. Likewise the redeemed are to be recompensed, not immediately when they die, but "at the resurrection of the just" (Luke 14:14).

The felicity of the redeemed will never be spoiled by the sight of the unsaved in fiery agonies. It is the false though popular doctrine of the immortality of the soul which has resulted in the interpretation of this passage as portraying the eternal destiny of the saved and the unsaved immediately when they die, causing a serious stumbling block to many would be Christians, and furnishing cause to atheists to ridicule the idea of a God, supposed to be omnipotent, just and kind, preserving human beings alive in fiery agony to all eternity, because of their sins of a brief life – for the most part not exceeding 100 years – in flesh on earth. If the doctrine of eternal torment is true, it constitutes the most dreadful news that ever fell on human ears.

But thank God, it is not true; God is Love. The redeemed will experience the unimagined intensity of His love, and its vast immensity, for Eternity; but His love is also just, and those not accounted worthy to obtain eternal life will be silenced at last in death; and "the dead know not anything."

"For the wages of sin is death; but the free gift of God is eternal life, through Jesus Christ our Lord."

Appendix
An Extract from Josephus:
"Discourse to the Greeks Concerning Hades"

Appendix: An Extract from Josephus

Discourse to the Greeks concerning Hades

Josephus's discourse to the Greeks concerning *hades* records what the Pharisees taught regarding the "intermediate state", "Abraham's bosom", etc.. It is a valuable insight into their teaching and is reproduced here, without comment. We trust that the reader may gain a fuller picture of how far their teachings strayed from what was taught in the Scriptures and how some modern days view have more in common with this extract than they do with the New Testament.

1) Now as to Hades, wherein the souls of the righteous and unrighteous are detained, it is necessary to speak of it. Hades is a place in the world not regularly finished; a *subterraneous* region, wherein the light of this world does not shine, from which circumstance, that in this region the light does not shine, it cannot be but there must be in it perpetual *darkness*. This region is allotted as a place of custody for souls, in which angels are appointed as guardians to them, who distribute to them *temporary punishments*, agreeable to every one's behaviour and manners.

2) In this region there is a certain place set apart, as *a lake of unquenchable fire*, whereinto we suppose no one hath hitherto been cast; but it is prepared for a day afore determined by God, in which one righteous sentence shall deservedly be passed upon all men; when the unjust and those that have been disobedient to God, and have given honour to such idols as have been the

vain operations of the hands of men, as to God himself, shall be adjudged to this *everlasting punishment,* as having been the causes of defilement; while the just shall obtain *an incorruptible* and never-fading *kingdom.* These are now indeed confined in Hades, but not in the same place wherein the unjust are confined.

3) For there is one descent into this region, at whose *gate* we believe there stands an archangel with an host; which *gate* when those pass through that are conducted down by the angels appointed over souls, they do not go the same way; but the just are guided to the *right hand,* and are led with hymns, sung by the angels appointed over that place, unto a region of *light,* in which the just have dwelt from the beginning of the world; not constrained by necessity, but ever enjoying the prospect of the good things they see, and rejoice in the expectation of those new enjoyments which will be peculiar to every one of them, and esteeming those things beyond what we have here; with whom there is no place of toil, no burning heat, no piercing cold, nor are any briers there; but the countenance of the *fathers* and of the just, which they see always smiles upon them, while they wait for that rest and eternal new *life in heaven,* which is to succeed this region. This place we call *The Bosom of Abraham.*

4) But as to the unjust, they are dragged by force to the *left hand* by the angels allotted for punishment, no longer going with a good-will, but as prisoners driven by violence; to whom are sent the angels appointed over them to reproach them and threaten them with their terrible looks, and to thrust them still downwards. Now those angels that are set over these souls, drag them into the neighbourhood of hell itself; who, when they are hard by it, continually hear the noise of it, and do not stand clear of the hot vapour itself; but when they have a nearer view of this spectacle, as of a terrible and exceeding great

prospect of fire, they are struck with a fearful expectation of a future judgment, and in effect punished thereby; and not only so, but where they see the place (or choir) of the *fathers* and of the just, even hereby are they punished; for a *chaos* deep and large is fixed between them; insomuch that a just man that hath compassion upon them cannot be admitted, nor can one that is unjust, if he were bold enough to attempt it, pass over it.

5) This is the discourse concerning Hades, wherein the souls of all men are confined until a proper season, which God hath determined, when he will make a resurrection of all men from the dead, not procuring a transmigration of souls from one body to another, but raising again those very bodies, which you Greeks, seeing to be dissolved, do not believe (their resurrection): but learn not to disbelieve it; for while you believe that the soul is created, and yet is made immortal by God, according to the doctrine of Plato, and this in time, be not incredulous; but believe that God is able, when he hath raised to life that body which was made as a compound of the same elements, to make it immortal; for it must never be said of God, that he is able to do some things and unable to do others. We have therefore believed that the body will be raised again; for although it be dissolved, it is not perished; for the earth receives its remains, and preserves them; and while they are like *seed*, and are mixed among the more fruitful soil, they flourish, and what is sown is indeed sown *bare grain*; but at the mighty sound of God the Creator, it will sprout up, and be raised in a *clothed* and *glorious* condition, though not before it has been dissolved and mixed (with the earth). So that we have not rashly believed the resurrection of the body; for although it be dissolved for a time on account of the original transgression, it exists still, and is cast into the earth as into a potter's furnace, in order to be formed again, not in order to rise again such as it was before, but in a state of purity, and so as never to be destroyed anymore; and to every body shall its own

soul be restored; and when it hath **clothed itself** with that body, it will not be subject to misery, but, being itself pure, it will continue with its pure body, and rejoice with it, with which it having walked righteously now in this world, and never having had it as a snare, it will receive it again with great gladness: but as for the unjust, they will receive their bodies not changed, not freed from diseases or distempers, nor made glorious, but with the same diseases wherein they died; and such as they were in their unbelief, the same shall they be when they shall be faithfully judged.

6) For all men, the just as well as the unjust, shall be brought before *God the word;* for to him hath the *Father committed all judgment;* and he, in order to fulfil the will of his Father, shall come as judge, whom we call *Christ.* For Minos and Rhadamanthus are not the judges, as you Greeks do suppose, but he whom *God even the Father hath glorified;* CONCERNING WHOM WE HAVE ELSEWHERE GIVEN A MORE PARTICULAR ACCOUNT, FOR THE SAKE OF THOSE WHO SEEK AFTER TRUTH. This person, exercising the righteous judgment of the Father towards all men, hath prepared a just sentence for every one, according to his works; at whose judgment seat when all men, and angels, and demons shall stand, they will send forth one voice, and say, **JUST IS THY JUDGMENT**; the rejoinder to which will bring a just sentence upon both parties, by giving justly to those that have done well an *everlasting fruition;* but allotting to the lovers of wicked words *eternal punishment.* To these belong the *unquenchable fire,* and that without end, and a certain fiery *worm never dying,* and not destroying the body, but continuing its eruption out of the body with never-ceasing grief; neither will sleep give ease to these men, nor will the night afford them comfort; death will not free them from their punishment, nor will the interceding prayers of their kindred profit them;

for the just are no longer seen by them, nor are they thought worthy of remembrance; but the just shall remember only their righteous actions, whereby they have attained *the heavenly kingdom,* in which there is no sleep, no sorrow, no corruption, no care, no night, no day measured by time, no sun driven in his course along the circle of heaven by necessity, and measuring out the bounds and conversions of the seasons, for the better illumination of the life of men; no moon decreasing and increasing, or introducing a variety of seasons, nor will she then moisten the earth; no burning sun, no Bear turning round (the pole), no Orion to rise, no wandering of innumerable stars. The earth will not then be difficult to be passed over, nor will it be hard to find out the court of Paradise, nor will there be any fearful roaring of the sea, forbidding the passengers to walk on it; even that will be made easily passable to the just, though it will not be void of moisture. Heaven will not then be uninhabitable by men: and it will not be impossible to discover the way of ascending thither. The earth will not be uncultivated, nor require too much labour of men, but will ring forth its fruits of its own accord, and will be well adorned with them. There will be no more generations of wild beasts, nor will the substance of the rest of the animals shoot out any more; for it will not produce men, but the number of the righteous will continue, and never fail, together with righteous angels, and spirits (of God), and with his word, as a choir of righteous men and women that never grow old, and continue in an incorruptible state, singing hymns to God, who hath advanced them to that happiness, by the means of a regular institution of life; with whom the whole creation also will lift up a perpetual hymn from *corruption to incorruption,* as glorified by a splendid and pure spirit. It will not then be restrained by a bond of necessity, but with a lively freedom shall offer up a voluntary hymn, and shall praise him that made them, together with the angels, and spirits, and men now freed *from all bondage.*

7) And now, if you Gentiles will be persuaded by these motives, and leave your vain imaginations about your pedigrees, and gaining of riches and philosophy, and will not spend your time about subtleties or words, and thereby lead your minds into error, and if you will apply your ears to the hearing of the inspired prophets, the interpreters, both of God and of his word, and will believe in God, you shall both be partakers of these things, and obtain the good things that are to come; you shall see the ascent into the immense heaven plainly, and that kingdom which is there; for what God hath now concealed in silence [will be then made manifest], *what neither eye hath seen, nor ear hath heard, nor hath it entered into the heart of men, the things that God hath prepared for them that love him.*

8) *In whatsoever ways I shall find you, in them shall I judge you entirely*; so cries the END of all things. And he who hath at first lived a virtuous life, but towards the latter end falls into vice, these labours by him before endured, shall be altogether vain and unprofitable, even as in a play, brought to an ill catastrophe. Whosoever shall have lived wickedly and luxuriously may repent; however, there will be need of much time to conquer an evil habit, and even after repentance his whole life must be guarded with great care and diligence, after the manner of a body, which, after it hath been a long time afflicted with a distemper, requires a stricter diet and method of living; for though it may be possible, perhaps, to break off the chain of our irregular affections at once, - yet our amendment cannot be secured without the grace of God, the prayers of good men, the help of the brethren, and our own sincere repentance and constant care. It is a good thing not to sin at all; it is also good, having sinned, to repent, - as it is best to have health always; but it is a good thing to recover from a distemper. *To God be glory and dominion for ever and ever. Amen.*

****

Other Works by
William Campbell

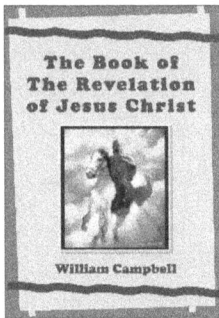

The Book of
The Revelation
of Jesus Christ

William Campbell

The
Prophecies
of Daniel

William Campbell

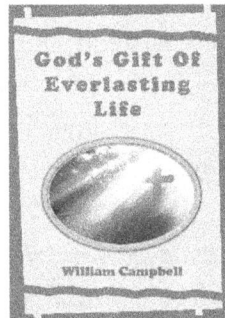

God's Gift Of
Everlasting
Life

William Campbell

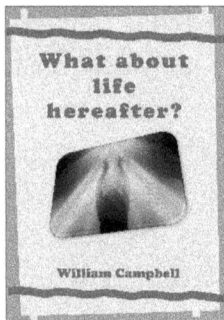

What about
life
hereafter?

William Campbell

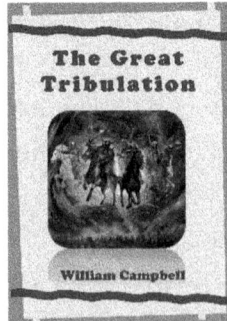

The Great
Tribulation

William Campbell

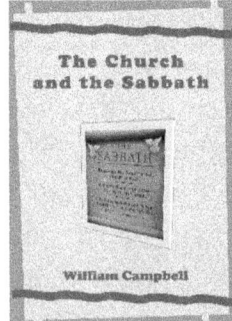

The Church
and the Sabbath

William Campbell

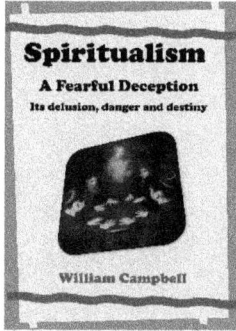

Spiritualism
A Fearful Deception
Its delusion, danger and destiny

William Campbell

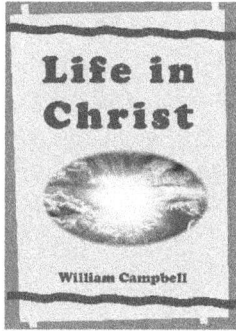

Life in Christ

William Campbell

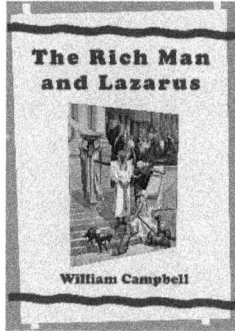

The Rich Man and Lazarus

William Campbell

The Book of The Revelation of Jesus Christ

The Prophecies of Daniel

God's Gift Of Everlasting Life

What about life hereafter?

The Great Tribulation

The Church and the Sabbath

Spiritualism: A Fearful Deception

Life in Christ

The Rich Man and Lazarus

For further information on these titles

**The Open Bible Trust,
please visit**

www.obt.org.uk

About the Author

William Campbell was the minister at the Church of Christ, West Street, Auckland, New Zealand. He was a great student of the Word and spoke and write mainly on salvation, conditional immortality and prophecy. This book was first written in 1945 and was reprinted in 1959.

For a list of some of the books published by The Open Bible Trust, please visit

www.obt.org.uk/books

Further Reading on ... The Rich Man and Lazarus

If you have found this book by William Campbell interesting and helpful, then we recommend that you read:

The Rich Man and Lazarus: the intermediate state
By E W Bullinger

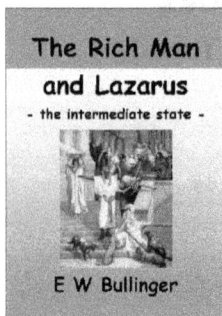

It is the author's contention that when dealing with the subject of what happens at death, it is important that Christians confine themselves to what the Bible has to say and turn neither to experiences nor to tradition. Experiences differ greatly and often contradict each other.

Also, some traditional Christian doctrines have more in common with the teachings of the Pharisees than with those of our Lord Jesus Christ and what is in the Bible. This is true of Luke 16:19-31, *The Rich Man and Lazarus*.

With an extensive use of both Scriptural and traditional sources, Dr. Bullinger places the evidence before the reader. As a result, Christians will be able to make up their own minds, and many will find this publication helpful and informative. Some may be surprised to learn just how much of the traditions of the Pharisees influenced early Christianity, and how some still permeates Christian thought today.

****

For further information on this publication and the ones on the next page

**The Open Bible Trust,
please visit**

www.obt.org.uk

Other Books on Hell and Conditional Immortality

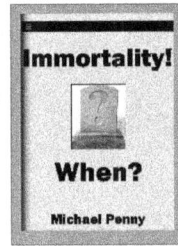

Asleep in Christ by Helaine Burch

Death! Fearing it or facing it? by Michael Penny

Hell and Judgment in the Book of Revelation by Colin Sweet

Immortality! When? by Michael Penny

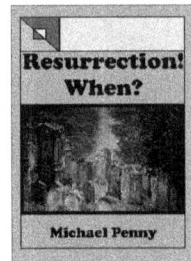

The Life and Soul of Mortal Man by Charles Ozanne

The Path to Immortality by Rowland Wickes

The Resurrection of the Body by E W Bullinger

Resurrection! When? by Michael and Sylvia Penny

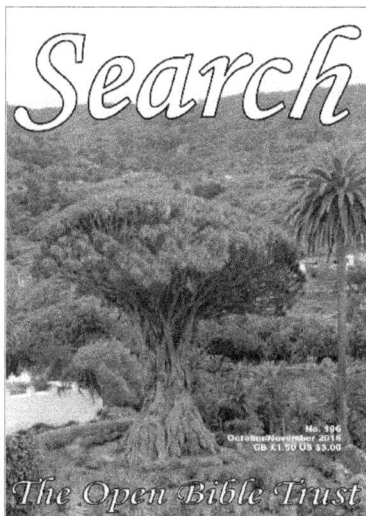

About this book

The Rich Man and Lazarus

So why did the poor man fare so well in the afterlife? It says nothing about him having faith in God!

And why did the rich man fare so badly? Is says nothing about him ***not*** having faith in God!

What was Christ teaching in "The Rich Man and Lazarus"? Certainly not asceticism, for if he was, we all, in the rich industrialised societies, are doomed!

You cannot preach the gospel of salvation by grace through faith from Luke 16. So what was Christ teaching?

The answer to that question is just what this thorough and informative book deals with, and the author[5] shows that the punch line of what Christ said is at the end of the account, aimed at his opponents, the Pharisees.

Publications of The Open Bible Trust must be in accordance with its evangelical, fundamental and dispensational basis. However, beyond this minimum, writers are free to express whatever beliefs they may have as their own understanding, provided that the aim in so doing is to further the object of The Open Bible Trust. A copy of the doctrinal basis is available on **www.obt.org.uk** or from:

THE OPEN BIBLE TRUST
Fordland Mount, Upper Basildon,
Reading, RG8 8LU, GB

www.ingramcontent.com/pod-product-compliance
Lightning Source LLC
Chambersburg PA
CBHW070544030426
42337CB00016B/2337